MARK TWAIN? WHAT KIND OF NAME IS THAT?

A Story of Samuel Langhorne Clemens

Robert Quackenbush
MARK TWAIN? WHAT KIND OF NAME IS THAT?
A Story of Samuel Langhorne Clemens

Simon and Schuster Books for Young Readers
Published by Simon & Schuster Inc., New York

SIMON AND SCHUSTER
BOOKS FOR YOUNG READERS
Simon & Schuster Building
Rockefeller Center
1230 Avenue of the Americas
New York, New York 10020
Copyright © 1984 by Robert Quackenbush
SIMON AND SCHUSTER BOOKS FOR YOUNG READERS
is a trademark of Simon & Schuster Inc.
Manufactured in the United States of America

10 9 8 7 6 5
10 9 8 7 6 5 4 3 2 1 ((Pbk)

Library of Congress Cataloging in Publication Data
Quackenbush, Robert M.
    Mark Twain? What kind of name is that?
    SUMMARY: The life of the famous humorist whose
numerous occupations included printer's apprentice,
steamboat pilot, gold miner, frontiersman, and reporter.
    1. Twain, Mark, 1835–1910—Biography—Juvenile litera-
ture. 2. Authors, American—19th century—Biography—
Juvenile literature. 3. Humorous, American—19th century
—Biography—Juvenile literature. [I. Twain, Mark,
1835–1910. 2. Authors, American. 3. Humorists]   I. Title.
PS1331.Q32 1984   818′.409 [B] [92] 83-19086
ISBN 0-671-66294-5   ISBN 0-671-69439-1 (Pbk)

Samuel Langhorne Clemens—river pilot, gold miner, frontier reporter, humorist, and this nation's best-loved author—claimed that two important events took place on November 30, 1835. One was the appearance in the night sky of Halley's Comet—an event that comes only once every seventy-five years—and the other was his birth in Florida, Missouri. Sam loved telling jokes and playing tricks. He claimed that he couldn't remember what his first lie was, but he told his second lie when he was only nine days old. He had pretended that a diaper pin was sticking him, and he'd hollered as loud as he could. This brought him extra loving attention—until his trickery was found out, that is. Sam's mother thought he might get hit by a bolt of lightning one day, on account of all the mischief he caused as he was growing up in Hannibal, Missouri, with his older brother Orion, his older sister Pamela, his younger brother Henry, and nineteen cats.

9

The cats belonged to Sam's mother. But Sam treated them as though they were his. All his life he liked to keep cats around him. His fondness for them caused folks in Hannibal to wonder if he were a cousin to the cat. After all, didn't he claim to have nine lives like a cat because that was how many times he had been rescued from drowning? And like a cat, wasn't he always in some kind of mischief, especially with that wayward friend of his, Tom Blankenship? Tom slept in the broken-down barn behind Sam's house. Many an evening he would give a shrill catcall and Sam would come sliding down a drain pipe. Then together they would sneak around the village till dawn, looking for a cure for warts or for treasure supposedly buried by a gang of robbers. During the day, Sam and Tom would include some of their friends in their mischief. One of the things they did was to roll boulders down a hill. One time a huge boulder narrowly escaped crushing a wagon and driver. Right then, the boys decided it was time to stop. That night, during a flash thunderstorm, lightning bolts struck all around. Sam was sure they were meant for him. He covered his head with his bed covers and promised to behave. But by morning all was forgotten, and he was back to his old tricks.

11

SAMMY SURE TAKES THINGS TO EXTREMES, SOMETIMES.

When Sam was eleven, his father died of pneumonia. To help support the family, Sam quit school and went to work for a printer. He learned to set the metal letters—called type—from which newspapers and advertisements are printed. Soon he became a first-class typesetter. Then his brother Orion returned from living in St. Louis where he had also been a typesetter. Orion bought a newspaper called the Hannibal *Journal*, and Sam became his assistant. Whenever Orion had to go out of town, Sam was left in charge. One time when his brother was away Sam thought of a way to get more readers for the paper. He asked the nosiest people in town to tell him all the gossip. Then he printed what they said. This did increase business and pleased the readers—all except those whose names appeared in the "hot" items. But when the angry readers came to complain—one of them armed with a shotgun— they found only an innocent-looking boy in charge. Luckily Orion returned in time to smooth things over and to put an end to Sam's mischief for a while.

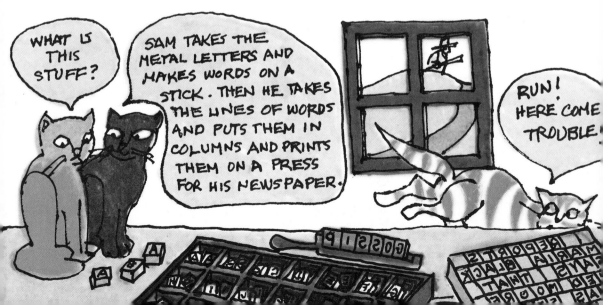

But Sam had decided he liked to write. He sent short funny stories to a large Eastern newspaper, and they were published. By the time he turned seventeen, he realized that he knew as much about newspapers as his brother did. So he decided to go off on his own. He went to work as a typesetter for newspapers in St. Louis, New York, Philadelphia, and back in St. Louis. After that he went to work again with Orion, who was now living in Keokuk, Iowa, and then he worked in Cincinnati. Printing newspapers became his college education, just as it had for Benjamin Franklin and Abraham Lincoln. But after ten years of working as a printer, Sam got restless. He wanted to try something else, like finding riches in South America. In April 1857, at the age of twenty-one, he boarded a steamboat to New Orleans, where he planned to take a ship to the Amazon. But as soon as Sam was on the Mississippi, he forgot about South America. On the wide river he felt that he was home. He suddenly knew what he wanted to do more than anything else. He wanted to become a riverboat pilot.

Sam begged the pilot of the riverboat, Horace Bixby, to teach him everything he knew. Bixby agreed, providing that Sam paid him five hundred dollars—one hundred right away and the rest to be paid out of Sam's first earnings. Gladly, Sam agreed, and Bixby proceeded to teach him the Mississippi from St. Louis to New Orleans—twelve hundred miles of points, bends, snags, bars, lowheads, crossings, landings, and constant change. One day near the end of his training, Sam had a bad scare. The men below were shouting that the water was too shallow, although Sam was sure that it was plenty deep. Bixby was nowhere in sight. Sam wondered what to do. He was shaking from head to foot. Just then Bixby appeared to tell him that it had all been a test of Sam's skill—the big boat had been in deep water all along. From then on Sam knew he could trust his knowledge of the river.

17

Bixby made a first-class riverboat pilot out of Sam. Soon Sam was earning two hundred and fifty dollars a month—an enormous sum at the time. He piloted the river for four and a half years, and he couldn't have been happier. Then America was suddenly thrust into a Civil War. Steamboat travel was coming to an end. Sam decided he would have to give up doing what he loved best and join an army. But which one? In June 1861, he decided to join a group of fourteen men near Florida, Missouri, who planned to fight for the South. He was given an old mule, an older rifle, blankets, a frying pan, a suitcase, a homemade quilt, boots, a coil of rope, and an umbrella. Sam soon found out that nobody in the group knew anything about military training and they all wanted to be officers. But one thing they did teach him a lot about was retreating. And after two weeks, retreating is what he did—for good.

18

When Sam quit the army, he learned that his brother Orion had been appointed secretary of the Nevada Territory. Sam asked if he could go along as Orion's assistant. Orion agreed and Sam paid their way on the first stagecoach heading west. When they got to Nevada, Sam set about trying to find riches by digging for silver. He didn't find much, so in his spare time he wrote funny stories and letters. He sent them to a newspaper—the *Daily Territorial Enterprise* at Virginia City, Nevada. Before long, he received a letter offering him a job as city editor of the paper for twenty-five dollars a week. Without a moment's hesitation, Sam dropped his pick ax and went to Virginia City. Whenever he wrote something factual for the paper, he used his own name—Sam Clemens. But whenever he wrote something funny, he used a pen name he had thought up. It was Mark Twain—a call used by rivermen to mean "safe water," a depth of two fathoms (twelve feet). "Mark Twain" began to grow famous, and his pay rose to $40 a week.

Suddenly Mark Twain's reputation as a humorous writer was sweeping across the country. This happened mainly through a series of hoaxes he published. Twain's most famous hoax was a funny story he made up about some miners uncovering a three-hundred-year-old petrified man. The so-called "news item" went on to say that the stone figure sat thumbing its nose. The story became national news, and some news reporters completely missed the fact that the story was a joke. They told their own versions of it as though it were the truth. From all over, magazines and newspapers poured into Virginia City with different accounts of the story. Some of the local officials got very angry, because they thought people were laughing at their town. Still, Sam kept on making up funny newspaper articles like this one and the officials became so outraged that they threatened to throw him in jail. Sam decided he had better get out of town fast. He took the first stagecoach to San Francisco.

In San Francisco, Twain worked for a while for a newspaper called the *Morning Call*. But the things he wrote about the city government made the politicians angry, and Twain fled to the gold fields in Sacramento Valley. Swapping stories before a wood stove in December 1864, he heard a Western version of an ancient Greek tale about a frog-jumping contest. Soon Twain wrote his own version about the stranger who fills his rival's frog with quail shot to keep it from jumping. The story, called "The Celebrated Jumping Frog of Calaveras County," was printed in newspapers from coast to coast. Mark Twain became known as "The Wild Humorist of the Pacific Slope." The attention his story received encouraged Twain to give up his quest for gold and do more writing. He persuaded a newspaper, the *Sacramento Union,* to send him to the Sandwich Islands, as Hawaii was then known, to write a series of stories about sugar plantations.

While in Hawaii, Twain wrote a news article about an exciting event—the burning at sea of the clipper ship *Hornet*. The article was reprinted in newspapers everywhere, and Twain became known as a news reporter. But he wanted more than that. Upon his return from Hawaii, everyone told him that writing for newspapers was one thing, but his work must appear in a magazine if he wanted to be known as a real author. So Twain reworked the *Hornet* story as "Forty Three Days in an Open Boat" and sent it to *Harper New Monthly Magazine*. Then he sat back and waited. At last his story appeared in the December 1866 issue of the magazine. But Mark Twain had not become a famous author—the magazine had listed his name as "Mark Swain." And so, Twain remained in California for a while, where he met Artemus Ward, a noted humorist and lecturer. Ward urged Twain to give lectures too. In San Francisco, Twain gave his first lecture to a packed house. And no wonder! The poster at the theater said, "Doors open at 7 o'clock. The Trouble to begin at 8 o'clock."

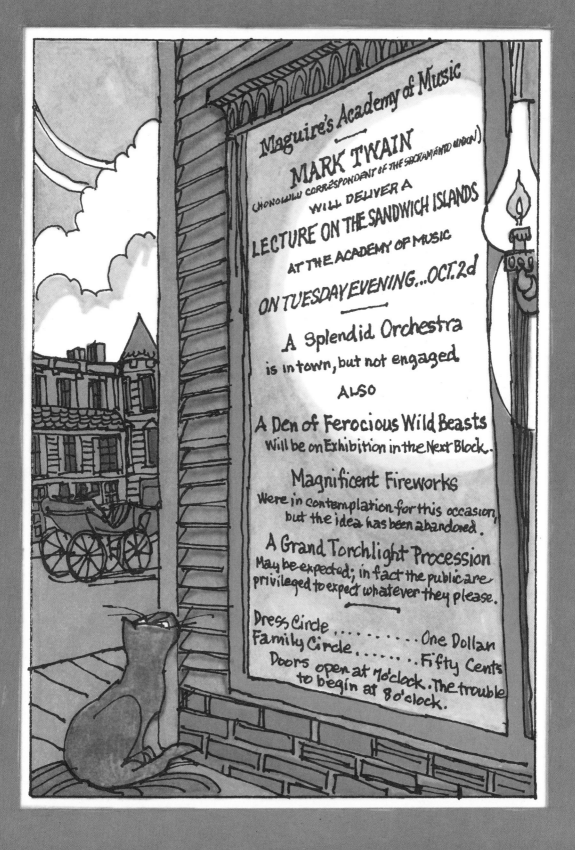

When Twain was thirty-one, he went to New York. He arranged to have "Jumping Frog" and other stories published in a book. Then he had a new idea. He would travel to Europe on the sidewheel steamer *Quaker City,* and he would write about the famous sights of the Old World as an American saw them. A California newspaper agreed to pay for his five-month tour of Europe and the Holy Land with a sizeable group of United States tourists. When Twain returned home in November 1867, his articles about his travels had made him a national celebrity. The articles were published in a book called *Innocents Abroad;* it became an instant bestseller and the most popular book of humor ever published up to that time. It included side-splitting jokes about the ancient monuments and the tourists. For example, Twain told how some of his tour group had teased an Italian guide. When the guide proudly showed them a statue of Columbus, the Americans pretended that they had never heard of Columbus. It was clear to the folks in Hannibal and to everyone who knew him that Sam Clemens, now known as Mark Twain, was still his same mischievous self.

29

On his travels Twain had become acquainted with Charles Langdon, from Elmira, New York. Langdon showed his writer friend a
miniature portrait of his sister Olivia. Twain couldn't wait to meet
her. He remained in the East after the voyage to court and marry
"Livy," his companion and editor for the next thirty-five years.
After their wedding on February 2, 1870, they lived for a while in
Buffalo. Then they settled in Hartford, Connecticut. They built an
enormous house that cost a fortune. Critics said it looked like a
steamboat. Here Mark Twain, famous author, father of three
daughters, and proud owner of nearly a dozen cats, enjoyed
seventeen of his happiest and most productive years. During this
time, Livy smoothed the rough edges of her husband and his prose.
For example, while Twain thought that his character Tom Sawyer
would say that patent medicines roasted the "guts" of his aunt's cat,
Livy changed the word to "bowels." Often Twain argued over
things like this, but Livy usually won.

30

Although Mark Twain's best books were published while he lived in Hartford, most of the actual writing was done during summer visits to the Langdons' Quarry Farm near Elmira, New York. On the hillside some distance from the house, a small eight-sided study was built for him. It looked like a ship pilot's house atop a steamboat, and this is where he worked. In 1876, *The Adventures of Tom Sawyer*, based on Twain's boyhood experiences in Hannibal, was published. In 1882 came *The Prince and the Pauper*, a fictional tale in which Prince Edward of England exchanged clothes and lifestyles with a street urchin. *Life on the Mississippi*, a colorful account of the steamboat era and the science of piloting, was published in 1883. It was followed in 1885 by *The Adventures of Huckleberry Finn*, about a runaway boy (modeled after his boyhood friend Tom Blankenship) and an escaped slave floating on a raft down the Mississippi. And in 1889 came *A Connecticut Yankee in King Arthur's Court*, about an enterprising Yankee mechanic who awakens in Camelot and tries to modernize life in the Middle Ages. These are only a few of Twain's published works, which include forty books and countless stories and essays.

Mark Twain earned a lot of money from his books. However, he also lost thousands of dollars by investing in all kinds of wild ideas and inventions, such as a complicated automatic typesetting machine, a self-pasting scrapbook, and a belt-like contraption called an adjustable clothes strap. Twain went to live in England for nine years because it was less expensive. But even so, he came face to face with a $150,000 debt. He immediately set out on a world-wide lecture tour for a year, paid his debts, and returned to the United States. When he came home in 1900, he was given a hero's welcome. People loved and respected the man who had gone to work at age eleven to help his family, who had written so many wonderful books, and who had worked hard to pay back all the money he owed. Twain spent his last years in a house called Stormfield at Redding, Connecticut. Naturally there was a cat in every room. And if you are wondering who were the favorites, they were Beelzebub, Blatherskite, Apollinaris, and Buffalo Bill.

35

EPILOGUE

On April 20, 1910, Halley's Comet appeared again in the night sky. Mark Twain had often said that he had come to this earth with the comet and that he would leave with it. True to his word, the next day he died. The world mourned for the author who had loved to poke fun at society and events. But for all his jokes, Mark Twain had a deep feeling for humanity and a hatred for injustice. This came through in his work and is what truly endeared him to the world. His best-loved books—*The Adventures of Tom Sawyer, The Adventures of Huckleberry Finn,* and *Life on the Mississippi*—continue to be translated into many foreign languages. In their pages are found Twain's family and the playmates of his boyhood in marvelous tales that tell us something about ourselves. The characters come to life in that golden era before the closing of America's frontier. And the laughter goes on.

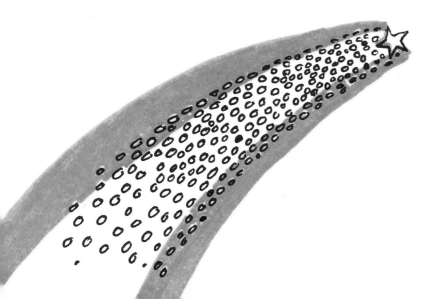